SPEED ZONE

SUPERFAST TRAINS

by Alicia Z. Klepeis

Ideas for Parents and Teachers

Pogo Books let children practice reading informational text while introducing them to nonfiction features such as headings, labels, sidebars, maps, and diagrams, as well as a table of contents, glossary, and index.

Carefully leveled text with a strong photo match offers early fluent readers the support they need to succeed.

Before Reading

- "Walk" through the book and point out the various nonfiction features. Ask the student what purpose each feature serves.
- Look at the glossary together. Read and discuss the words.

Read the Book

- Have the child read the book independently.
- Invite him or her to list questions that arise from reading.

After Reading

- Discuss the child's questions. Talk about how he or she might find answers to those questions.
- Prompt the child to think more. Ask: Why can some trains go so fast? Can you think of any other superfast vehicles?

Pogo Books are published by Jump!
5357 Penn Avenue South
Minneapolis, MN 55419
www.jumplibrary.com

Library of Congress Cataloging-in-Publication Data

Names: Klepeis, Alicia, 1971- author.
Title: Superfast trains / by Alicia Z. Klepeis.
Description: Minneapolis, MN: Jump!, Inc., [2022]
Series: Speed zone
Includes index. | Audience: Ages 7-10
Identifiers: LCCN 2020054209 (print)
LCCN 2020054210 (ebook)
ISBN 9781645279709 (hardcover)
ISBN 9781645279716 (paperback)
ISBN 9781645279723 (ebook)
Subjects: LCSH: High speed trains—Juvenile literature.
Magnetic levitation vehicles—Juvenile literature.
Railroad trains—Technological innovations—
Juvenile literature. | CYAC: High speed trains.
High speed ground transportation.
Classification: LCC TF1455 .K54 2022 (print)
LCC TF1455 (ebook) | DDC 625.2/3—dc23
LC record available at https://lccn.loc.gov/2020054209
LC ebook record available at https://lccn.loc.gov/2020054210

Editor: Eliza Leahy
Designer: Molly Ballanger

Photo Credits: cyo bo/Shutterstock, cover, 6-7, 16-17; pedrosala/Shutterstock, 1; Sakarin Sawasdinaka/Shutterstock, 3; noina/Shutterstock, 4; Christian Petersen-Clausen/Getty, 5; VCG/Getty, 8-9; Gregory_DUBUS/iStock, 10; Piti Sirisriro/Shutterstock, 11; Thierry Monasse/Getty, 12-13; Hitman H/Shutterstock, 14; Jose Manuel Revuelta Luna/Alamy, 15; KoreaKHW/Alamy, 18-19; The Asahi Shimbun/Getty, 20-21; Simon Tang/Shutterstock, 23.

Printed in the United States of America at Corporate Graphics in North Mankato, Minnesota.

TABLE OF CONTENTS

CHAPTER 1

MAGLEV TRAINS

All aboard! A superfast train is about to leave the station. It is the Shanghai Maglev in China. It is the fastest train people can ride. It reaches 268 miles (431 kilometers) per hour!

Shanghai Tran

This train doesn't rumble over tracks. It floats! It is a maglev train. Strong magnets are in the train and the rails. The magnets **repel** one another. This makes the train float above the rails.

magnet

The magnets also **propel** the train forward. How? Magnets ahead of the train pull it. Magnets behind the train push it.

DID YOU KNOW?

Since maglev trains don't touch the rails, there is no **friction**. This means the train can move faster.

maglev
test train

Engineers in China are working on an even faster maglev train. It is designed to reach 372 miles (599 km) per hour.

DID YOU KNOW?

Today it takes 5.5 hours to travel by train from Beijing to Shanghai. The new maglev train will take just 3.5 hours!

CHAPTER 2

POWER UP!

Not all fast trains use magnets. Many use **locomotives**. These work as large **engines** to pull the cars. The TGV in France is one example. TGV trains can go 186 miles (299 km) per hour.

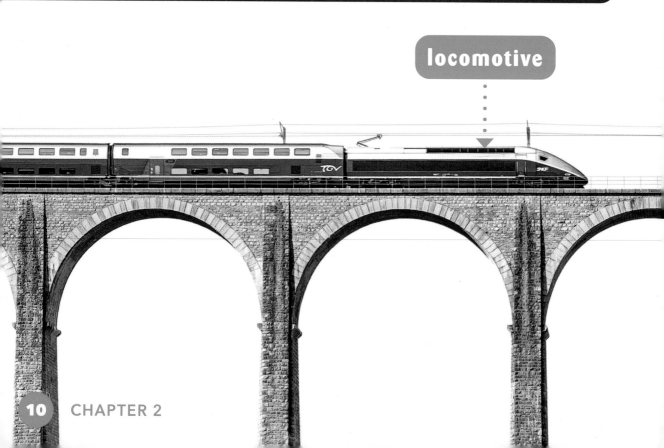

locomotive

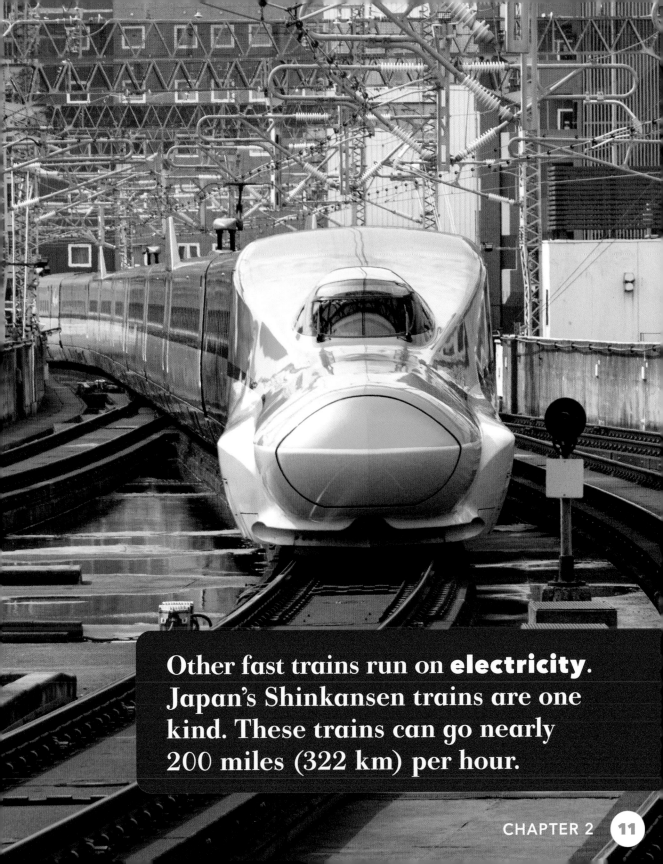

Other fast trains run on **electricity**. Japan's Shinkansen trains are one kind. These trains can go nearly 200 miles (322 km) per hour.

Electricity comes from wires above the tracks. A **pantograph** is on top of each train. This arm draws electricity from the wires to the train.

pantograph

CHAPTER 3

SUPERFAST DESIGNS

A train's design can help it go faster. Many fast trains have **aerodynamic** front cars. Their shapes reduce **drag**. One kind is called a bullet train. Its nose is shaped like a bullet.

nose

The Talgo 350 can go 217 miles (349 km) per hour. Its front car looks like a duck's beak. It cuts through the air.

Superfast trains are made with light materials. Why? It takes less power to **accelerate** trains that weigh less. Some trains have covers over their wheels. These help reduce drag, too.

wheel cover

TAKE A LOOK!

How fast do some of the fastest trains go? Take a look!

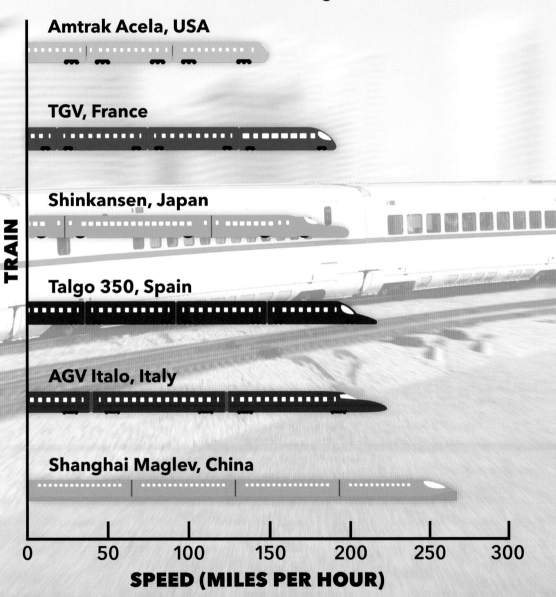

TRAIN

Amtrak Acela, USA

TGV, France

Shinkansen, Japan

Talgo 350, Spain

AGV Italo, Italy

Shanghai Maglev, China

0   50   100   150   200   250   300

SPEED (MILES PER HOUR)

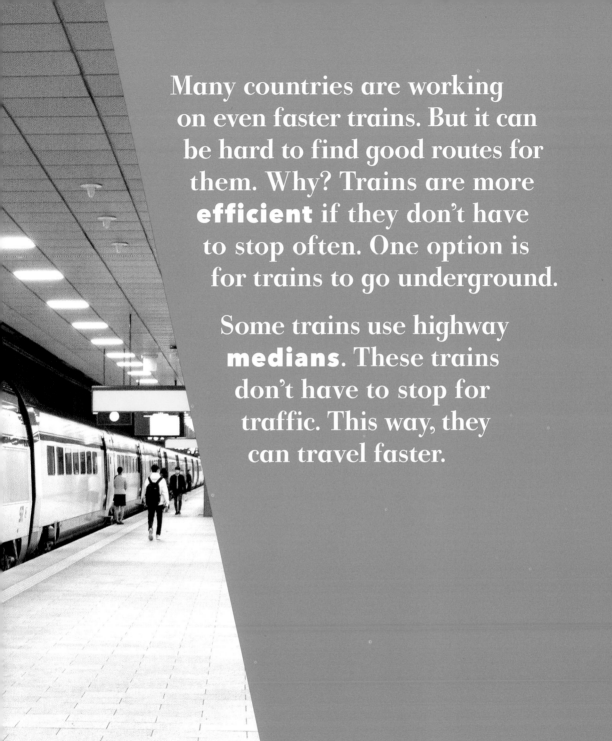

Many countries are working on even faster trains. But it can be hard to find good routes for them. Why? Trains are more **efficient** if they don't have to stop often. One option is for trains to go underground.

Some trains use highway **medians**. These trains don't have to stop for traffic. This way, they can travel faster.

A new maglev train is being tested in Japan. It can go 375 miles (604 km) per hour! People could ride it by 2027.

Engineers design faster and faster trains. What is the speed limit? Only time will tell!

DID YOU KNOW?

Hyperloop is a form of transportation that may be used in the future. People ride in pods. These travel inside a tube. They could go more than 600 miles (966 km) per hour!

maglev
test train

ACTIVITIES & TOOLS

BUILD YOUR OWN SUPERFAST TRAINS

Design two trains and see which goes faster with this fun activity!

What You Need:
- pencil or pen
- paper
- various recycled materials (shoeboxes, bottles, cardboard, etc.)
- glue or tape
- scissors

❶ Sketch two train designs that you think you can make and that you think would go fast. Try to have the shape of the two trains be somewhat different.

❷ Look around your home for materials you can use to make your trains. Your recycling bin is a good place to begin. A plastic bottle could make a lightweight but streamlined train car. Wooden skewers or straws work well as axles.

❸ Use the materials you find to build the trains you sketched.

❹ When both trains are done, line them up on the floor. At the same time, give them a push. Which one goes faster? Why do you think that is? Can you think of a way to make it go even faster?

GLOSSARY

accelerate: To move faster and faster.

aerodynamic: Designed to move through the air easily and quickly.

drag: The force that slows motion, action, or advancement.

efficient: Uses less energy to perform a task.

electricity: Power that is generated in large plants and distributed through wires.

engineers: People who are specially trained to design and build machines or large structures.

engines: Machines that make things move by using gasoline, steam, or another energy source.

friction: The force that slows down objects when they rub against each other.

locomotives: Engines used to push or pull railroad cars.

medians: Narrow strips of land that separate opposite sides of large roads.

pantograph: An arm or hook that transfers electricity to a train from overhead wires.

propel: To push something forward.

repel: To force away or apart.

INDEX

TO LEARN MORE

Finding more information is as easy as 1, 2, 3.

❶ Go to www.factsurfer.com

❷ Enter "superfasttrains" into the search box.

❸ Choose your book to see a list of websites.

FACT SURFER